YOUR KNOWLEDGE HAS

Bibliographic information published by the German National Library:

The German National Library lists this publication in the National Bibliography; detailed bibliographic data are available on the Internet at http://dnb.dnb.de .

Imprint:

Copyright © 2010 GRIN Verlag, Open Publishing GmbH
Print and binding: Books on Demand GmbH, Norderstedt Germany
ISBN: 9783640542819

This book at GRIN:

http://www.grin.com/en/e-book/144464/energy-efficiency-of-server-grids

Christina Herzog

Energy Efficiency of Server Grids

GRIN Publishing

GRIN - Your knowledge has value

Since its foundation in 1998, GRIN has specialized in publishing academic texts by students, college teachers and other academics as e-book and printed book. The website www.grin.com is an ideal platform for presenting term papers, final papers, scientific essays, dissertations and specialist books.

Visit us on the internet:

http://www.grin.com/

http://www.facebook.com/grincom

http://www.twitter.com/grin_com

Questions and Solutions of Energy Efficiency in the Server Grid
Technology

Table of Content

Abstract

According to the estimations the level of carbon emission in the sector of information and communication technologies triples by 2020[1]. This raised concern regarding the energy efficiency of the ICT devices and systems. Further we will discuss the guidelines and directives along which we can differentiate between technologies and their efficiency-level. These guidelines not only enable the customer of these services to attain a simple and easily manageable view on his consumption as technology user, but it also provides an evaluation system for local governmental and international regulators and projects. Then we examine the problem of energy efficiency in a specific field of the ICT, the server grids, as the demand for the services of this area is one of the fastest growing sections of the ICT sector. Than we rule out two possible ways of solving energy efficiency on the grids, and compare them. Finally in the conclusion we point out the main factors that make these solutions successful, and to which extent they match to our guidelines.

Key word: energy efficiency, information and communication technologies, energy awareness, server farms, server grids, network technologies

1. Introduction

The recent results of the studies of climate change scientists are more than alarming. The estimation of their new models shows that the pace and impact of global warming on human society and ecological environment might be even more devastating than it had been expected before. These studies claim that unless the emission of greenhouse gases is reduced to 20% under the level of 1990 by 2020, dramatic changes of the climate and the environment are inevitable[2]. Growing public and governmental

---

[1] SMART 2020: Enabling the low carbon economy in the information age
http://www.smart2020.org/_assets/files/03_Smart2020Report_lo_res.pdf

[2] Pachauri, R.K. and A. Reisinger (eds.)
(2007) Climate Change 2007: Synthesis Report. Contribution of Working Groups I, II and III to the Fourth Assessment Report of the Intergovernmental Panel on Climate Change, IPCC, Geneva, Switzerland.

concern regarding this issue has raised awareness to the impact of information and communication technology and its possible utilization in other areas.

The challenge of energy efficiency is the one contemporary technology engineering and design has to face. Though the innovations of information and communication technology (ICT) has tremendously reduced the costs and energy consumption of everyday life and business, through its amazing pace of growing in penetration and range the sector itself is consuming more energy than ever.

According to the reports of SMART 2020 the ICT sector - devices and services from PC's to telecom networks, and data centers- accounts for 8% of the electrical power used and around 2% of carbon emissions pf human race. Around the quarter of the carbon generated in this sector overall derives from the production of the devices, the rest comes from their usage. Though the growth of the penetration of these products and services in highly developed countries are not expected to be low, the growth in the following years will be inevitably tremendous in developing countries. By 2020, approximately a third of the future population will own a PC, respectively to the current rate of one in 50, 50% will have a mobile phone and 20% will have broadband Internet connection.

According to the estimation of these reports the level of carbon emission of this sector will triple by 2020[3]. These facts raised concern regarding the energy efficiency of the ICT devices and systems. Further we will discuss the guidelines and directives along which we can differentiate between technologies and their efficiency-level. These guidelines not only enable the customer of these services to attain a simple and easily manageable view on his consumption as technology user, but it also provides an evaluation system for local governmental and international regulators and projects. Then we examine the problem of energy efficiency in a specific field of the ICT, the server grids, as the demand for the services of this area is one of the fastest growing section of the ICT sector. Than we rule out two possible ways of solving energy efficiency on the grids, and compare them. Finally in the conclusion we point out the main factors that make these solutions successful, and to which extent they match to our guidelines.

---

[3] SMART 2020: Enabling the low carbon economy in the information age
http://www.smart2020.org/_assets/files/03_Smart2020Report_lo_res.pdf

2. Key actions and guidelines for the ICT sector

In the report of SMART 2020 an overview of five key actions regarding the energy efficiency of ICT sector and ICT influenced sectors has been drown, based on a throughout analysis of energy consumption patterns. The first step according to these guidelines is to standardize (S) the measure methods according which emission data and energy consumption can be transformed into information that makes technologies, products and services of a sector and across sectors comparable.

The second key factor is to monitor (M) energy consumption and emissions across the industry in real time, providing the data needed to optimize for energy efficiency. This factor allows that the formerly obtained standardized data is fully available and observable for all agents in the economy, not only in delayed aggregated stage but also in the moment of consumption. This allows the agents to reconsider and if needed reallocate their consumption and needs.

Accordingly, each step of usual business conduct (BUA - business as usual) should be possible to identify and be accountable (A) for its energy consumption and emission. This way, stages of higher emission can be located in the BUA of products and services.

Using the gained information we can rethink (R) how we can live, work, act in a low carbon economy, reducing our emission levels by optimizing efficiency and providing low carbon alternatives. Ultimately this set of technologies, designs, architectures and mind-sets will have the great impact to emerge a platform, where leading low carbon alternatives can be developed and implemented in the economy on large scale, transmitting (T) it to a greener society.

3. The challenge of the data center

According to the SMART2020 report one of the greatest challenges green IT has to face is the immense growth of server farms and server grids. These equipments store and make available vast amount of information at any given time the user requires it. To maintain this service these data centers needs storage devices, network plants, fans and cooling systems, power supplies, and an enormous amount of energy. The carbon footprint of these centers is expected to grow more than 7% a year, making it the most carbon-expansive component of the ICT sector.

Considering the guidelines above there are several ways to reduce the energy consumption of server farms at different stages of the complex working routine of the server grids. One of them is rationalizing the cooling system of the servers. Allowing the volatility of temperature to rise somewhat higher would save energy as well as instead of apply local cooling mechanism that identifies the overheated points of the server farm and cools only these points instead of big overall cooling systems. Another possibility on this area is to relocate server grids to colder regions so that less energy is needed to cool them down. Google implements this principle in an almost futuristic way. In its new pattern it describes a water-based data center, where the server panels, network resources and processing modules are all embedded in a ship, which anchors on open sea, using the breaking waves as energy source and cooling system alike.[4] A different angle of view to this problem is how to turn waste energy to useful energy. There are plans to heat nearby buildings to server grids by with the wasted heat of their local server farms.[5] Considering the question of cooling is essential for the future of ICT. By 2020 4% of the total energy consumption will be consumed by cooling systems for ICT devices and networks.

Besides the changing of the physical attributes of the hard drives, there is a huge potential of consume reduction in visualization. The basic idea of this concept is to use the unused capacities of hardware emerging from both the boom of computing performance and the idle periods due to the uneven demand of end-users. Virtualization is a pooling technology that "combines or divides computing resources to present one or many operating environments using methodologies like hardware and software partitioning or aggregation, partial or complete machine simulation, emulation, time-sharing, and others."[6]

Virtual machines that give the impression of using the physical machine but actually work only on the fragment of it were already in use in the 1960's. By then computing capacities were still very expensive and relatively rare, and virtual machines

---

[4] Clidaras, Jimmy ; et al. (2008) Water-Based Data Center http://appft1.uspto.gov/netacgi/nph-Parser?Sect1=PTO1&Sect2=HITOFF&d=PG01&p=1&u=%2Fnetahtml%2FPTO%2Fsrchnum.html&r=1&f=G&l=50&s1=%2220080209234%22.PGNR.&OS=DN/20080209234&RS=DN/20080209234
[5] A Greener Way? Grids and Green Computing in *GridBriefings Grid computing in five minutes (2009-7)*
[6] Nanda, Susanta;Chiueh, Tzi-cker: A Survey on Virtualization Technologies 2005 http://www.ecsl.cs.sunysb.edu/tr/TR179.pdf

made by time- and resource-sharing these capacities available for wider usage. These virtual machines were isolated and secure copy of the underlying system of them, and so all users could let their applications run and computing execute without risking of system collapse.

This technology has been forgotten with the technology development as computing resources became less and less scarce. Still in recent times as the demand extends rapidly and as this expansion has to face much less technological than raw material and energy resource boundaries the potential of the concept of virtual technology gained more attention and popularity. In the following section we will discuss two technologies based on the idea of virtualization technologies recently developed for the rationalization and energy efficiency of server grids.

4. Green Strategies of Grid: SymbioticSphere and Energy-Aware Reservation Infrastructure (EARI)

SymbioticSphere[7] is a biologically-inspired architecture design for data centers, which makes them capable to adapt dynamic environmental changes, survive partial system failures and reach energy efficiency. The concept of this system is based on the life cycle of bee colonies, where each server and platform is analogous to an individual bee, autonomously acting, interacting and adapting to changes of environment whereas server farms are designed to follow biological principles, such as natural selection, decentralization and symbiosis.

EARI on the other hand is based on the recognition that server farms have their capacity designed to satisfy the maximum task load of busy periods when the demand from the end-user side is the highest. According to this there are huge amounts of waste energy in idle periods mostly emerging from booting, shutting down, idle state consumption and when they are connected to the energy source but not actively operating. The designers intended to develop an optimal scheduling algorithm that

---

[7] Champrasert, Paskorn ; Suzuki, Junichi "A Biologically-Inspired Autonomic Architecture for Self-Healing Data Centers," Computer Software and Applications Conference, Annual International, pp. 103-112, 30th Annual International Computer Software and Applications Conference (COMPSAC'06), 2006

switches off the unused nodes, predict which nodes are to be used in the near future, and switches them on, and aggregate tasks to prevent too frequent on-off switches.[8]

Simulations show that these server grids are both capable of saving up to 50% of the energy on their platform.

Further along this chapter we will examine the design principles, the architecture and the working methods of these platforms with the aim of pointing out similarities and differences in their activities, so that we can better understand how these and analog platforms function.

4.1 Architecture of server grids:

The architecture of SymbioticSphere is designed to simulate the basic characteristics of the energy flow of our ecosystem. These basic attributes are, that the system gets light energy from one source (the Sun), which is converted to chemical energy by producers (e.g. plants), which is than the utilizable form of the energy for consumers (other species of the planet.) Whereas most of energy is used for self maintenance (e.g. metabolism, growth, actions), there is a remarkable amount of energy transfer between species.

In SymbioticSphere each user acts like a separate Sun and as like the sun the have disposal over unlimited amount of energy. Agents gain the energy it requires for its services from the user. They expand then energy for the platforms; in exchange they get computing resources. To model the energy transfer between species agents periodically transfer 10% of their energy to the platforms they are operating on, and platforms periodically gain energy from agents, and evaporate 10% of their energy level to the environment.

Each agent has attributes and a body. The attributes describe the services the agent provides, and hold information of the agent's ID and energy level. The body carries out the services of the agent, for example an agent may offer web services, and this way the body may contain web pages.

---

[8] Orgerie, Anne-Cecile; Lefevre, Laurent ; Gelas, Jean-Patrick "Save Watts in Your Grid: Green Strategies for Energy-Aware Framework in Large Scale Distributed Systems," Parallel and Distributed Systems, International Conference on, pp. 171-178, 2008 14th IEEE International Conference on Parallel and Distributed Systems, 2008

The platforms operate on network hosts and manage agents. Each platform has attributes and runtime services. The attributes provide information about the platform's ID, its energy level, and its so called health level. Health level is a combination of the accessible resources from a platform's network host it operates on, and the age of this host. This information describes the stability and resource availability of the host for agents and platforms.

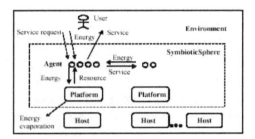

Figure 1 Architecture of SymbioticSphere[9]

The architecture of the EARI is based on the Grid5000 platform. This is easily controllable and adaptable experimental equipment with around 3400 processors. The operation of the Grid is very specific, as each user can reserve some nodes in advance, when they expect to need computing resources. During the reservation time the nodes are entirely dedicated to the user, the user has all the rights, even root rights during this period. In this system each user is connected to a portal where he submits his reservation. The portal sends these reservations to the scheduler, which collects and validates them, building up the schedule agenda, that states the execution list of tasks or reservation. The scheduler allocates and manages the resources according to this agenda. On each resource, which can be nodes, routers, etc. there is an energy sensor set up to monitor the energy properties of that resource. The data of these sensors are collected by the infrastructure, which than computes energy saving recommendation to the portal, so

[9] Champrasert, P. and Suzuki, J. 2006. Towards Green Grids: A Biologically-Inspired Adaptive Architecture for Power Efficient Server Farms. In *Proceedings of the international Conference on Autonomic and Autonomous Systems* (July 19 - 21, 2006). ICAS. IEEE Computer Society, Washington, DC, 39. DOI= http://dx.doi.org/10.1109/ICAS.2006.63

giving feedback to the user of the energy consumption of his past reservation, this way influencing his choice for reservations and scheduling these reservations. It is also the task of the infrastructure to decide which resources should be on, and which resources should be turned off.

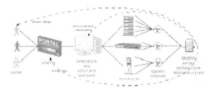

Figure 2 Architecture of Grid5000[10]

The most evident difference between these architectures is the controlling and coordination of the system. SymioticSphere is a decentralized system with units that manage self-control over allocation of the resources, and the access to these resources is driven by natural selection. Energy efficiency this way is not a goal of the system but a by-product of its operation, as those units become more successful that manage their tasks with lower resources or supply more service for the user on the same level of resources. On the other hand in Grid5000 there is a super computer that is specifically added to the system to monitor the energy consume of the elements of the grid. This computer with the help of past experiences regulates the energy access of the units of the grid, and also gives "green advices" to the users.

This leads us to the second difference of these systems. In SymbioticSphere the user - except for his initial input of energy, which the agents requires from him to provide its service in exchange – never gets information or decision over the energy consumption of his computing assignment. The EARI on the contrary provides exact real-time information of the tasks running on the system, and computes future energy consumption scenarios for each new reservation. It provides green alternatives to the user so that he can re-schedule his reservations on to more energy-efficient times.

[10] Orgerie, A., Lefèvre, L., and Gelas, J. 2008. Save Watts in Your Grid: Green Strategies for Energy-Aware Framework in Large Scale Distributed Systems. In *Proceedings of the 2008 14th IEEE international Conference on Parallel and Distributed Systems* (December 08 - 10, 2008). ICPADS. IEEE Computer Society, Washington, DC, 171-178. DOI= http://dx.doi.org/10.1109/ICPADS.2008.97

4.2 Principles of behavior and the working methods

SymbioticSphere has two levels of operating principles both of which are inspired by principles ruling the ecological system. The first set of these principles acts on the level of the whole system. Some of these were already mentioned, here we collect and analyze them more thoroughly.

Decentralization allows scalability of the platforms/agents letting them to adapt their needs of resources to their task requirements by avoiding single bottleneck-points in their performance and avoiding central coordination of agents and platforms. As there is no central coordination, agents and platforms are able to perform autonomously. They detect their local environment in the network, and based on this perception they interact without any intervention. Agents and platforms store and consume energy for a living. Agents perform their services to gain energy and use energy to reach network and computing resources, while platforms are gaining energy from the agents to provide them those resources and for evaporating energy periodically. Differences of energy levels trigger natural selection among platforms and agents. Scarcity of energy on an agent or platform means that there is not enough demand for its services/resources, which causes the death of these units. Contrary, higher energy level means greater demand for services or resources, which allows this agent/platform to replicate itself to increase availability.

Platforms and agents are operating under dynamic environmental conditions. Agents migrate towards platforms that are able to provide them resources that they need for their services, platforms replicate themselves on hosts with higher resource availability. Thus desired system characteristics, like adaptability, sustainability, energy efficiency and reliability emerge from these collective behaviors and interactions; they are not present in the individual agents or platforms that coexist in a symbiotic relationship, one cannot survive without another. This provides higher energy efficiency by turning off network hosts that don't host agents.

On the unit level, platforms and agents are both carrying features of living creatures. They are able to replicate themselves in the presence of abundant energy, and they die of in energy starvation. The replicate agent gains half of the energy of its parent, and it's based on its parent's platform. If an agent dies the platform under it removes the

11

agent, and releases the resources it used. The child platform also gains half of its parent energy level, but it can be hosted by neighboring hosts, in case they are healthier (see above) than the current one. Dying platforms uninstall themselves and free all the resources it has used. Agents can also migrate to neighboring platforms if this platform has more available, not yet engaged resources than the parenting platform.

Each of these behaviors generate energy loss on the agents or platforms (except for the death behavior) to prevent them to perform these behaviors too often. When the energy level of a unit reaches the energy cost of a behavior the unit decides whether to perform this behavior based on the agent's perception of the local environmental circumstances.

In the system with the EARI the behavioral principles limits themselves only to the calculations of the super computer. These algorithms are split into two parts, one regarding the start-up time, and the other regarding the ending time of a reservation. To calculate these times the algorithms check the start and end times of other reservations on the agenda, and they check if it is possible to place the reservation before and after them. This way the algorithm finds several start and end times for a reservation, and checks for the one that minimize the energy consumption of it. Finally the results of all these calculations are delivered to the user, who gets the opportunity to choose the scheduling that fits his preferences regarding the timing and his energy consciousness.

The algorithms of the EARI try to allocate resource necessities in clusters. They make prediction of the next incoming reservation and on the resources that needs to be released for that. Than they compute through the time frame of the reservation whether it could be scheduled on operating resources or not. If it is possible the algorithms calculate the possibility of turning of the running but idle resources, and if the it is energy efficient the super computer turns off these. As we see the algorithms make estimations for the future by deriving information from the past. To improve these estimations there is a feedback built in the algorithms that measures the mistake by comparing *ex ante* estimations to *ex post* outcomes. These algorithms also have a load balancing system which ensures that the scheduler will not always use the same resources, along with a topology model of the grid that allows to schedule resources together that are geographically further from each other. These techniques prevent heat accumulation that reduces cooling costs.

The most important actor regarding the issue of energy efficiency remains the user in this system. The user decides if he accepts the green policy of the EARI, and if he is ready to reschedule his reservation.

5. Conclusions

As we have seen, these two grid platforms operate with a pool of resources. These pools are constantly filled with new resources which are not busy at the moment by locating them along the system. Then they evaluate the possibility of reallocate tasks on these reserves to utilize them, or to shut them off.

SymbiothicSphere doesn't require any decisions on the energy policy from the user. It relies fully on the present demand of the users, and the present state of the units. The history of last allocations and demands are irrelevant in this system, as the information on these is stored in the density and energy level of agents, platforms and hosts. Thus the system doesn't have to make any estimation regarding the future, as the units are only operating to provide their services and resources in exchange for energy. It establishes a stable system, where energy efficiency emerges in a decentralized manner purely from the behavioral "instincts" and "laws" of the system. Coordination and control are not needed in this system.

Whereas EARI controls centrally the system it's operating on, it collects and evaluates data, and makes estimations for the future, based on the history of reservations, estimations and mistakes of the past. It actively involves the user in the energy saving process, giving him more and less energy efficient alternatives for the same computing reservation.

Both platforms manage to fulfill the SMART2020 requirements. They find a standardized way to measure energy usage of different units, and they monitor their usage. All units, as well as computing demands from the user are accountable for their energy usage. These two attributes are more clearly fulfilled in the case of the centralized grid of EARI, which leads us to the last two conditions. It is undoubtedly this platform that urges the user to revise his energy needs and to transform them according to an energy aware computing policy.

Though the mind-set changing affect of actively involving the user to become energy aware, giving him energy saving options and allowing them to monitor his real-time consumption, has undeniable merits, but as we stated at the beginning of the analysis the two system in their most beneficial stages could both save around the same amount of energy. Further on energy efficiency doesn't apply for the super computer of the centralized system, whereas energy saving occurs on all nodes at the decentralized system.

Literature:

1, Pachauri, R.K. and A. Reisinger (eds.) (2007) Climate Change 2007: Synthesis Report. Contribution of Working Groups I, II and III to the Fourth Assessment Report of the Intergovernmental Panel on Climate Change, IPCC, Geneva, Switzerland.

2, SMART 2020: Enabling the low carbon economy in the information age
http://www.smart2020.org/_assets/files/03_Smart2020Report_lo_res.pdf

3, Clidaras, Jimmy ; et al. (2008) Water-Based Data Center
http://appft1.uspto.gov/netacgi/nph-
Parser?Sect1=PTO1&Sect2=HITOFF&d=PG01&p=1&u=%2Fnetahtml%2FPTO%2Fsrc
hnum.html&r=1&f=G&l=50&s1=%2220080209234%22.PGNR.&OS=DN/20080209234
&RS=DN/20080209234

4, A Greener Way? Grids and Green Computing in GridBriefings Grid computing in five minutes (2009-7)

5, Nanda, Susanta;Chiueh, Tzi-cker: A Survey on Virtualization Technologies 2005
http://www.ecsl.cs.sunysb.edu/tr/TR179.pdf

6, Champrasert, Paskorn ; Suzuki, Junichi "A Biologically-Inspired Autonomic Architecture for Self-Healing Data Centers," Computer Software and Applications Conference, Annual International, pp. 103-112, 30th Annual International Computer Software and Applications Conference (COMPSAC'06), 2006

7, Orgerie, Anne-Cecile; Lefevre, Laurent ; Gelas, Jean-Patrick "Save Watts in Your Grid: Green Strategies for Energy-Aware Framework in Large Scale Distributed Systems," Parallel and Distributed Systems, International Conference on, pp. 171-178, 2008 14th IEEE International Conference on Parallel and Distributed Systems, 2008

8, Champrasert, P. and Suzuki, J. 2006. Towards Green Grids: A Biologically-Inspired Adaptive Architecture for Power Efficient Server Farms. In Proceedings of the international Conference on Autonomic and Autonomous Systems (July 19 - 21, 2006). ICAS. IEEE Computer Society, Washington, DC, 39. DOI=
http://dx.doi.org/10.1109/ICAS.2006.63

www.ingramcontent.com/pod-product-compliance
Lightning Source LLC
Chambersburg PA
CBHW031235050326
40689CB00009B/1619